ALONE ON A DESERT ISLAND

ALONE ON A DESERT ISLAND

Ginny McReynolds

Illustrated by Charles Shaw

RAINTREE PUBLISHERS
Milwaukee • Toronto • Melbourne • London

Library of Congress Number: 79-22144

1 2 3 4 5 6 7 8 9 0 84 83 82 81 80

Printed and bound in the United States of America.

Library of Congress Cataloging in Publication Data

McReynolds, Ginny.
  Alone on a desert island.

  SUMMARY: A biography of the man whose
experiences as a castaway on a desert island in the
Pacific inspired Defoe's Robinson Crusoe.
  1. Selkirk, Alexander, 1676-1721 — Juvenile
literature. 2. Adventure and adventurers—
England — Biography — Juvenile literature.
[1. Selkirk, Alexander, 1676-1721. 2. Adventure
and adventurers] I. Shaw, Charles, 1941-
II. Title.
G530.S42M32   910'.92'4 [B] [92]   79-22144
ISBN 0-8172-1571-9 lib. bdg.

CONTENTS

CHAPTER 1

Left Alone

The sun had been up only an hour, but there were already eight men gathered on the deck of the old ship. They were all very different from one another—except for one thing. Each was seeking adventure. And that was what brought them to the deck of the old *Cinque Ports* at this early hour on September 5, 1703.

The men were privateers. Privateers were private citizens who were hired by European countries in the 1700s to sail on private ships and fight enemy ships. Because they weren't really sailors, they were sometimes criticized for being too much like pirates. Pirates were not hired by the government. They would attack any ships they came upon and steal their gold.

Of the eight men on the deck of the *Cinque Ports*, only one was talking.

"Why, we can't sail around Cape Horn on this," he said. "There are supposed to be thirty or forty of us. We'll be much too cramped. Three days out at sea and we'll be ready to string each other up. We ought to have a larger, better ship or refuse to leave. I just can't see fighting those bloody Spanish on an old, broken-down ship like this."

"Is that right?" a loud voice questioned from behind. "What is your name?"

"Selkirk, sir. Alexander Selkirk."

"Well, Mr. Selkirk, I am Lieutenant Thomas Stradling, your superior. *This* is the ship we will be sailing on. If the size or condition of the ship bother you, you have plenty of time right now to get off. But there will be no more discussion and no more threats. Do you understand?"

Selkirk grumbled something under his breath.

"Do you understand, Selkirk?"

"Yes, sir," Selkirk answered.

The *Cinque Ports* sailed at 9:00 A.M. It was headed for the South Seas. It began by traveling south through the Atlantic Ocean and then around Cape Horn in South America, up the South American coast and into the Pacific. Its goal was to stop Spanish ships that were carrying gold. The Spanish were England's bitter enemies, and England had commissioned the *Cinque Ports* to sail against any Spanish ships.

As the days passed, Selkirk was not any easier to get along with. He hated the conditions on the ship and continued to try to get the other crew members to complain. To make matters worse, Lieutenant Stradling drank heavily, which irritated Selkirk no end. Every time Stradling saw Selkirk, he was talking to someone about the crowded conditions, the poor food, and Stradling himself. Several of the men on board agreed with Selkirk enough to listen to him, which made Stradling's job of keeping everyone in line quite difficult.

As the *Cinque Ports* rounded Cape Horn and began its journey into the Pacific, it encountered the Spanish. The battle began immediately. Cannonballs were flying. The men of the *Cinque Ports* took their posts and fired endless rounds at their enemy. When part of the Spanish ship was sinking, and many of the Spaniards had been killed, they waved a small white surrender flag. The *Cinque Ports* won that battle for England, but their ship, too, was in bad shape.

The *Cinque Ports* could sail no further without emergency repairs. Checking the maps, Stradling found the Juan Fernandez Islands directly north, off the coast of Chile. They reached the island of Mas a Tierra without any trouble, and they anchored there to work on the boat.

After a few days, Stradling decided the ship was ready to sail. Selkirk, once again, began to grumble.

"That ship is not ready to sail," he said.

"Selkirk, it *is* ready to sail and it *will* sail. Tomorrow morning."

"It may sail tomorrow morning, *sir*. But it will sail without me. I would rather be left on this desert island than go on in a leaky ship with an ignorant commander."

"Fine, Selkirk. You may remain here. It will certainly be a favor to the rest of us. Maybe you can even talk a few of your friends into staying with you."

When the ship was ready to sail the next morning, Stradling did not ask Selkirk to change his mind. In fact, he totally ignored him. Selkirk, pretending to be very happy about his decision,

stayed away from the others as they were preparing to leave. He had been unsuccessful in getting anyone else to join him on the island.

Just as the last man was boarding the ship and pulling up anchor, Selkirk thought of his home in Scotland. He remembered his parents, his six brothers, and his little village, Largo. He would probably never see any of that again if he remained on the island.

"Stop," he cried out, running out into the water. "Stop, Stradling, I've changed my mind." But Stradling just waved.

"Have fun, Selkirk. Maybe you can cause trouble among the rats. I'm sure you can get a few of them to go along with you."

Selkirk continued to wade out into the water. Now it was serious. Tears began to roll down his

cheeks. "Please Stradling, stop." But it was too late. Even if he had started to swim, he could never catch up with the *Cinque Ports*. The winds were perfect and carried the ship away from Mas a Tierra quickly.

Selkirk fell to his knees weeping. "Oh, God," he cried. "I will never see my home again."

CHAPTER 2

A Hard Life

Standing alone on Mas a Tierra, Selkirk thought his life was over. He knew he would never see his home or his family again, and he longed to be aboard the *Cinque Ports* on his way back to the British Isles.

Little did Selkirk know, however, that he had been right about the *Cinque Ports*. Stradling sailed another 1,000 miles up the South American coast. The ship was in such bad condition by that time, however, that it ran aground off Peru.

As Stradling and the crew were examining the ship and trying to decided what to do, their future was decided for them. A Spanish ship came upon them and took them prisoner.

Stradling and his men begged to be freed, but the Spanish paid no attention to them. Instead, the Spanish tortured the men of the *Cinque Ports* and finally threw them into chains.

Selkirk did not know what had happened to his

fellow seamen, but at that point he might have preferred their chains to his future on Mas a Tierra.

Things had never been very easy for Alexander. His quick temper and inability to adjust had caused him problems all his life. His behavior on the *Cinque Ports* with Lieutenant Stradling was very much like his behavior throughout his life.

Born in 1676, his real name was Alexander Selcraig. He was the seventh son in the Selcraig family and grew up in Largo, a tiny fishing village in the County Fife, Scotland. Throughout his childhood he was hot-headed, and became very upset whenever things didn't go his way. He was always in trouble and was known throughout the community as a troublemaker.

But Alexander's mother had different plans for him when he was born. She considered it a lucky sign that he was her seventh son. She thought he was destined to have a fine, successful life.

Yet, early on, her hopes for Alexander were unfulfilled. As a young boy he would start fights with others when they disagreed with him. He often stirred up trouble among the other children in his family, and usually did just what he wanted to do when he wanted to do it.

By the time he was nineteen, Alexander had one major accomplishment to his name. He had been kicked out of town for beating up some of his rivals. If that wasn't bad enough, the fight occurred in the middle of church services.

His family was disgraced. Alexander was the main topic of conversation among the members of the community. His parents were furious with him. His life in Largo was over.

"Father, I know I have made everyone very unhappy," he said. "Now I, too, am unhappy. The only choice I have is to go far away. I am signing up with a Dutch ship which is sailing to the West Indies. I will be far enough away that I cannot possibly cause my family any more heartbreak." Alexander's father agreed this would be the best thing for his son to do.

The young man sailed with the Dutch for the next six years. He finally grew very homesick for Largo and his family, so he returned. After only a few weeks at home, there were problems again. One night the Selcraigs were all sitting around the table after dinner. One of Alexander's brothers asked him to tell some stories about his adventures on the high seas. Everyone was glad to have Alexander back, and he was glad to have so much attention.

But, the peace and quiet was short-lived. When he began to tell his story, his oldest brother interrupted. When his brother interrupted a second time, Alexander had all he could take. He grabbed him by the shirt collar and told him to keep his mouth shut.

That was all it took to get things going. When it ended ten minutes later, Alexander had slugged three of his brothers and his father.

Because his behavior was so bad the kirk, or national church of Scotland, demanded he make a public apology. Alexander considered this and decided it would be better to leave town.

The only real choice he had was to sign on with a ship of privateers who were sailing the high seas looking for enemy ships. That very day, while walking through town, Alexander eyed a notice asking for able-bodied men to join up with the *Cinque Ports*. The pay seemed good and Alexander was something of a pirate anyway. That was it.

He walked down to the dock, asked to sign the *Cinque Ports* roster and began thinking about all the adventure he was about to experience. When it came time to actually sign his name, Alexander paused a moment. Then, instead of Alexander Selcraig, he wrote Alexander Selkirk. He had brought enough embarrassment to his family, he thought. He did not want to risk bringing them any more shame from his life of privateering.

And so it was that Alexander Selkirk joined the crew of the *Cinque Ports*, looking for adventure and excitement and, perhaps, some money. What he got, instead, was more trouble and a very strange life on Mas a Tierra.

CHAPTER 3

The Ship Is Gone

After the *Cinque Ports* sailed away, Alexander turned and looked at the island. He couldn't believe this was happening to him. The island was beautiful and green and lush, there was no doubt about that. Tall palm trees covered the interior of the island, and everywhere there were thick, green plants and delicate, fragrant flowers. But the beauty did not make Alexander any happier.

For several hours he sat on a rock next to the water and watched the horizon line for boats. There was nothing. He cried, tried to sleep, watched for boats some more, and hoped that any moment Stradling would return for him.

As the sun began to set, Alexander started to feel cold. He was wearing only wool britches and a lightweight shirt. He remembered there was a coat in the sea chest he had brought from the ship. Never believing Stradling would take him at his word, he had carelessly thrown a few things into the chest that morning. It didn't occur to him at the time to take things that might actually help him survive on the island. The coat warmed him, and he remained on the rock, looking through the chest at what he had actually brought with him.

The chest contained only three things. The coat. A small leather pouch of tobacco. A copy of the Holy Bible. Irritated at his carelessness, he threw the Bible and the tobacco back into the chest and stood up.

"I will search the island," he said, "and find a warm place to make a bed. Then, in the morning, I will be rested and ready when a ship comes to rescue me. Stradling will be back, I know it. If

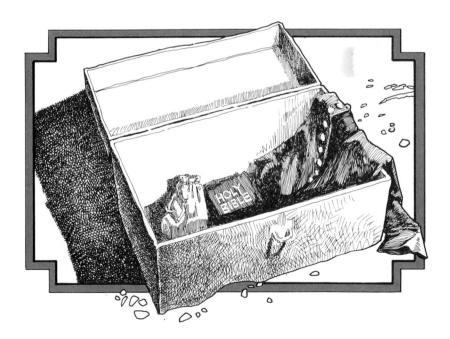

he doesn't come himself he will send a passing ship."

At that moment, as Selkirk turned to walk toward the trees, he heard a thundering sound coming toward him on the right. He looked up and saw ten huge, pig-like creatures galloping in his direction.

"Oh my dear God," he shrieked, and he ran as fast as he could to the nearest tree. He climbed with all of his strength to get out of the way of these wild beasts.

Catching his breath, Alexander looked down. The savage pigs were all charging around under the tree waiting, he thought, for him to come down. In the distance he could see some fierce-looking goats ramming their heads together, pounding their hooves noisily on the ground.

"Dear God," Alexander said aloud, tears running down his cheeks. "Save me from this and I will never behave badly again. I will listen to what others have to say. I will go to the kirk daily and beg your forgiveness. I will honor the wishes of my parents. But please, send someone to save me. I will never survive on this island."

As dawn was breaking, Alexander awoke. He was surprised he had slept. Most of the night he felt too afraid and too cold to actually get to sleep. Then, whenever he heard a sound in the distance, he was sure it was a ship. He worried that no one would see him in the dark.

Alexander sat in the tree for another hour before getting up the nerve to climb down. It was his growing hunger that finally forced him back to the ground. He caught a fish by hand that morning and ate it raw—a most unpleasant meal. But his meals were all like that for the first eight months.

Alexander remained close to the water at all times during those first months. His eyes were nearly always on the horizon watching for ships. He ate mainly fish, turtles, berries, and coconuts. He gathered enough wood each day to build a little fire at night. The fire kept him warm and he thought it also might attract any ships that passed.

He hated every waking moment. He did very little exploring because he was afraid of what he might find. The wild pigs charged up once or twice a day, but usually they seemed as afraid of him as he was of them.

One of Alexander's biggest problems those first few months was fresh water. He knew that drinking seawater would make him sick, so everyday he searched slightly further for a fresh water pool or spring. He wouldn't allow himself to go very far, though, so he had to settle for digging deep into the earth for a little fresh water, usually mixed with mud.

It took him only a few days to smoke the small

supply of tobacco he had brought with him, and he refused to look at the Bible for two or three months, feeling God had betrayed him by making him live on this island.

Mainly Alexander sat on a rock or in a little trench he had dug for himself, watching the horizon, thinking about how terrible his life was. The only thing distracting his thoughts during the day were the rats coming up and nibbling at his toes. One morning he awoke to find a large rat sitting on his chest sniffing at his beard.

Hunting for food each day was something Alexander hated, because it forced him to take his eyes off the horizon. So he would try to find

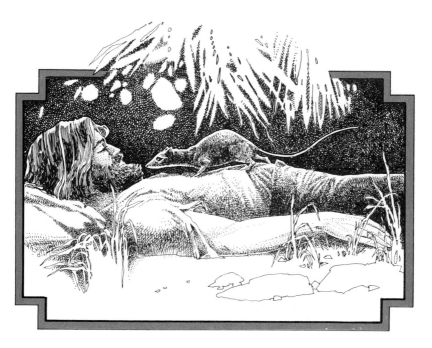

enough food one day to last him through the next few. Yet, he was never able to hide it from the rats, who were eating more than Alexander.

No matter what Alexander did, he was always thinking of how to get off the island. He thought of everything. He considered swimming until he could reach a boat to rescue him. He even thought he might set fire to the whole island in order to attract someone in a passing boat. All he wanted was to get off the island. He couldn't seem to make himself think about what to do *on* the island.

He thought if he actually accepted his life on the island—if he really started *living* on it—he would never be saved.

"I must get off," he said to himself one afternoon. "I will die or go crazy if I continue to stay here. I must create a way to be saved or to save myself."

CHAPTER 4

A New Life

Two or three months after he said that, Alexander was still on the island. He had grown so sick of eating fish and turtles, he would go whole days without eating. Then he would find some berries or old coconuts and would eat enough of those to stop the gnawing in his stomach. He ate everything he found immediately, since it seemed impossible to fight the growing rat population. They were everywhere now.

"I must go further into the island to look for food," he said, "or I will surely die."

The next day, carrying some large, sharp rocks for protection, he headed into the island. For eight months he had been hearing the strange sounds of the animals on the island. The memory of those noises frightened him. His first encounter with any life, though, was with some animals that looked like cats. They were different from the cats he had seen in Scotland—bigger,

with longer, larger teeth, wilder-looking eyes, and sharper claws. He decided they were just cats, though, which had come from passing ships.

When the cats saw him, they ran, frightened by this two-legged creature carrying large rocks. Once hidden in the bushes, they began making a low, crying sound. Alexander recognized the noise as the one that had been frightening him for months. He felt relieved to know it was coming from these cats.

He found more berries and coconuts on that trip into the island and continued to explore further each day. He was actually looking forward to waking up every morning to head in a new direction. In a week he had seen every inch of the island. He had found nothing so frightening he couldn't master it.

He had seen several herds of wild goats and many more cats. One afternoon he found a small, freshwater pool which was about four feet wide and two feet deep. If he was careful, he thought, that water would last him a while. He later found three more pools, and his search for fresh water was no longer a problem.

Deep in the island one day, he came upon a small cave dug in the side of a hill. He worked on the cave for a week, digging and molding and scraping, until he had created a home for himself. He returned to his original trench, gathered up his things and headed back to the cave. On the way, he realized something important.

"I am living here now," he said. "I have accepted the fact that this is my home. I will probably never live anywhere else." It surprised him and saddened him. But it also made him feel safe. He was learning the island and surviving on it. He was part of the island.

The cats were as curious about Alexander as he was about them. They would sit outside his cave in the morning waiting for him to come out. When he did they would always run into the bushes and watch him from there.

He, on the other hand, would try to coax them out. He would place little bits of fish on the ground near the bushes. They would always come out to eat, but would run back quickly. They were beginning to trust him, though, and they rarely left the area near his cave.

One day he placed the food farther from the bushes and made a little trail of food leading right into his cave. The cats ignored the food for one full day. The next day two of them walked right up to him, ate the last piece of food and walked slowly back to the trees.

In a few more weeks, he had them actually eating out of his hand. Some even slept in the cave with him at night. He liked having the cats because they were friends for him. They walked with him when he went hunting for food, and they sat with him by the fire at night. Mainly, he liked having the cats because they solved the problem he was having with the rats.

Although he still dreamed of being rescued, that was not all he thought about each day, as he had in those first few months. Instead, he busied himself with other activities. If he was doing something besides thinking about being rescued, he decided, the time passed more quickly. He kept track of the time by making marks on a tree near his cave.

Every morning he would make one small mark near the bottom of the tree. When he had made thirty of those, he made a larger mark higher up,

indicating how many months had passed. When he had twelve month marks, he made one large mark right in the middle of the tree. This told how many years he had been on the island.

Alexander's life became easier as he learned to work with what he had on the island. For example, the many palm trees were filled with coconuts. One day, while he was eating some of the soft, sweet meat of the coconut, he got an idea. He scraped the rest of the fruit out of the shell and filled the shell with water. It made a perfect cup. This helped him with eating and with gathering water.

He also found part of an old iron hoop that had

come off a ship. He pounded, bent, and sharpened the hoop and soon had made himself a knife. This allowed him to do more real hunting for food. He became quite a hunter and finally, with the proper weapon, mastered the goats.

From one goat he could get a great deal of meat, as well as skins, which he stitched together with an old nail and strings and grass. Alexander used these materials to make clothing to protect himself from the weather.

With his new-found confidence, Alexander returned to his faith and began reading the Bible daily. He felt this made him stronger and kept him from going crazy. He also believed it would be his faith, alone, that would bring someone to rescue him.

Another activity Alexander occupied himself with was a game he made up with the cats. One evening, sitting by the fire after dinner, he was petting two of the cats. He offered them each a little goat meat and then, as they were ready to take it, he pulled it away, getting them to do a little dance. He would move the meat in front of them and they would move quickly back and forth. He practiced this little game over the next few months. Finally he had most of the cats trained to dance before they got fed.

One day in January, more than four years after Alexander had stepped off the *Cinque Ports*, he was near the edge of the island doing one of the things he did every day. He would build a small fire in some rocks near the shore. He had learned to tell which direction the winds were blowing and he would fix the fire so it burned slowly and made a lot of smoke. The smoke, he hoped, would attract a ship that might be sailing near the island.

Late that afternoon, back in his cave, Alexander was stretched out next to the cats reading the Bible. Suddenly he heard a loud commotion and ran to see if the pigs were disturbing the goats again. It was the pigs, all right, but the goats were nowhere in sight. Alexander looked around to see what was causing the pigs to get so excited.

CHAPTER 5

Goodbye to the Island

2092724

He looked toward the water and was stunned. There, within his view, was a ship.

Was it heading toward the island? It was so far away that he could not tell which way it was heading. At first he just stood there, shocked. It was the first ship he had seen in over four years.

"Ship. A Home," he yelled. After so many years with only the cats, most of what he said was very short. He even made up a few words of his own, since he was living in his own world.

He jumped up and down waving his arms wildly in the air. "Here!" he screamed. "Save 'Xander. Save me!" The ship was moving very slowly. Alexander still could not tell if it was coming toward him or not.

As it grew dark he built up his fire, hoping to attract their attention. The boat seemed to be getting no closer, but it was not getting further

away either. Perhaps they have dropped anchor for the night, he thought.

"I'll be here," he said, and made a bed for himself that night near the rocks where he sat that very first day four years and four months before.

Alexander slept only an hour all night, making sure, always, that the fire was bright. When it began to die, he would gather more wood. By morning, eleven of Alexander's cats had gathered around him, wondering what was happening to their master. They had never seen him behave so strangely.

When Alexander awoke at dawn, he looked up immediately to see what had happened to the ship. His greatest hopes were fulfilled. The ship was headed toward the island. Within a couple of hours it had anchored, and two men were wading toward him.

"Hey, mate," they said, with a British accent. "We saw your fire. Stranded, eh?"

"A home," Alexander answered.

The man speaking looked questioningly at Alexander. "I'm Captain Woodes Rogers," he said. "This is Trenton Gladstone."

Alexander held out his hand. His fingernails were long and his hands were thin and weathered-looking. "'Xander Kirk," he said.

"Well, gather your gear mate and we'll take you aboard," Rogers replied. As Alexander ran into

the island to get his things, Rogers and Gladstone
watched him.

"Strange fellow, isn't he?" Gladstone asked.

"Quite a suit he's wearing. He looks wilder
than those skins' first owners. But, it looks like
he's been here quite a while, and we can certainly
use another hand on board."

With that, Alexander appeared again and they
all waded out to the ship. He was carrying his
knife, his sea chest, his coconut cup, his Bible,
and his favorite cat.

On board, Alexander met Roger's five other
crew members, who all looked at this thin, hairy,

bearded creature much the same way Alexander had looked at the wild pigs his first night on the island.

Though he was very grateful to be on board the *Duke* and on his way home, it took Alexander several weeks to adjust. He trimmed his beard and his hair, washed with some soap and water, and even regained his ability to speak correctly by listening to the other men.

In a funny way, Alexander missed his life on the island. His days there had been his own. For the first time in his life, he had been the boss. He was in charge of everything that happened. Nearly everything, that is. He never could control those wild pigs.

But he was very glad to be with people again, and realized that his time on the island had calmed him down a little. "Maybe that is why I had to stay there so long," he said to one of the men one day, "to learn to control myself."

Once Alexander had adjusted and could speak normally again, the men on the ship were fascinated with his stories about his adventures on the island. He became a kind of a hero on the ship.

It was three years before this ship returned to England. During that time Alexander became even more of a hero in the battles against the Spanish. He proved himself to be very skillful. Once, when Rogers captured a Spanish ship, he put Alexander in command of it. In addition to the command of the ship, Alexander was given a large amount of the money and gold on board.

Yet, even though Alexander Selkirk had returned to a normal life, he still showed some signs of having lived alone on a desert island for four years. He continued dancing with his cat and really preferred being alone to being with others.

CHAPTER 6

Another New Life

When Selkirk finally returned to England, he had quite a surprise waiting for him. Journalists from all over wanted to interview him about his adventures on Mas a Tierra. No one could believe he had survived the elements and returned to tell about it.

One of these journalists was a man named Daniel Defoe. Defoe had been writing for many years but had never really made his mark as a journalist. Everyone loved a story about an adventure at sea and Defoe saw this as a chance to write something really big. He interviewed Selkirk and, instead of writing his account in a newspaper, he decided to make it a novel. He renamed the castaway Robinson Crusoe and told an exotic, adventurous story of a man enduring great difficulties on a desert island.

Robinson Crusoe made Defoe's career. It became famous and made Defoe a well-known

novelist. Robinson Crusoe is a character every-one knows. But Alexander Selkirk is a little-known man who lived out the rest of his life alone.

After so many interviews that he was sick of telling the story, Alexander returned to his fami-ly's home in Largo, the town where he had been known as a troublemaker. He was again talked about. But this time it was because of his strange habits. Wherever he went, he had several cats trailing behind him.

When he tried to fit into life in Largo he had as hard a time as when he was a troublemaker. This time, though, it was for a different reason. Now he felt moody and depressed, and it was difficult for him to adjust to so many people and so much activity.

To feel more comfortable, Alexander moved from his family's house out into the garden. He built himself a small cave there, much like the one he had lived in on Mas a Tierra.

At first he felt better just having a more private, quiet house. He was able to go out during the day and come home to a house that felt comfortable. But he became more and more secluded. Finally, he rarely came out. He would stay indoors for days on end seeing no one but the many alley cats who had found a home with him.

He spent endless hours teaching little dances to these cats and his days seemed very much like his days on the island.

After several months of this, he knew what he was doing was not good for him. He knew he had to get out in the world and live a regular life. He wished he could just stay in the cave with the cats, but he forced himself out into the world.

Joining the navy seemed like a good idea. He could be on the sea, which he loved. And, he would not have the hustle and bustle of the town.

It was on the sea that Alexander contracted a fever. His ship was sailing off the coast of Africa, and several of the men went ashore. While there,

they were exposed to a fever, which they gave to others on board. Alexander became very sick and finally died. He was buried at sea.

When his family was told he was dead, they went out to the cave to gather up his things. They found only his sea chest and his coconut drinking cup. His cup was later placed in the Edinburgh Antiquarian Museum, where it was mounted on a silver pedestal.

Alexander Selkirk had a life of problems. As a young man he was quick-tempered and hard to live with. He caused trouble everywhere he went—even on board the *Cinque Ports*. He was unable to cope with people around him.

That problem was solved for him when he was left alone on Mas a Tierra. For the next four years and four months Alexander Selkirk was forced to create a life for himself on the island. He resisted that force for the first eight months, but finally adjusted so well that it was difficult for him to return home and be happy.

He did have some successful days at sea and, though people never knew him as the real Robinson Crusoe, it was Alexander Selkirk who conquered the desert island. It was Alexander Selkirk who proved, finally, that he was a strong, brave, capable man.